All You Wan

Aura

Ravindra Kumar, Ph D

(Swami Atmananda)

New Dawn

NEW DAWN
a division of Sterling Publishers (P) Ltd.
A-59, Okhla Industrial Area, Phase-II, New Delhi-110020
Tel : 6916209, 6916165, 6912677, 6910050; Fax: 6331241
E-mail : ghai@nde.vsnl.net.in
www.sterlingpublishers.com

All You Wanted to Know About - Aura

ISBN 81 207 2350 3
Reprint 2001, 2002

Published by Sterling Publishers Pvt. Ltd., New Delhi-110020.
Lasertypeset by Vikas Compographics, New Delhi-110020.
Printed at Shagun Composer, New Delhi-110029.

Contents

Preface

'Aura' enables us to perceive the soul and to interpret its various appearances. Anything having an atomic structure will have an aura, which is a 'field of energy' surrounding it. Holy people have a large field of energy and they have generally been portrayed with a luminous halo around their heads, either white or golden in colour. Colours in an aura around the body clearly tell about the physical, mental, emotional and spiritual condition of the person.

This book gives the details of auric studies conducted at the Academy of Kundalini Yoga and Quantum Soul. Thanks are due to William Henry Belk for useful discussions, and to Jytte Larsen for help in computing facilities.

Introduction

Most of us experience aura in our daily lives, whether we know about it or not. It is a thin pulsating field around the human body and its colours can be seen by anyone with sustained practice and patience. My own experiences in life have convinced me about the powers of clairvoyant sight, to see an aura. I have been seeing my own aura within for several years, the colours changing according to inner development and evolution, and also according to the emotions and the state of mind at different times.

A large number of people in the world are not yet convinced about the powers of aura. A blind man can say to us that there is no such thing as 'physical sight' and if we say that we have it, we are fooling ourselves. We can simply reply, "Excuse me, I have it, and no power on earth can make me say otherwise, since I have daily experiences of seeing with my eyes." The same thing can be said about auras, and for that matter, about other paranormal powers. One can easily acquire the power of seeing auras with regular practice and patience. It is easy to learn to see auras if you take a relaxed and playful approach. One has to create a situation similar to the 'twilight zone' which exists when you are about to slip in or out of sleep. It is then that the paranormal just happens. This is how you see visions.

The history of aura began in ancient times when halos were seen around the heads of holy persons from India, Greece, Egypt and Rome. These halos depicted auras in luminous or golden colour (Figure 1). The 'vital energy' which constitutes

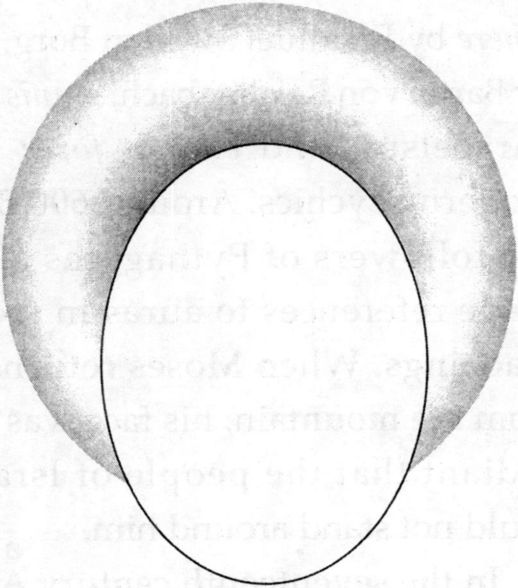

Figure 1
Halo in Ancient Pictures

the aura is called *prana* by Hindus, *mana* by Polynesians, *animal magnetism* by Mesmer, *spiritual sphere* by Emanuel Sweden Borg, *od* by Baron von Reichenbach, *munis* by Paracelsus, and *etheric force* by modern psychics. Around 600 BC, the followers of Pythagoras also made references to auras in their teachings. When Moses returned from the mountain, his face was so radiant that the people of Israel could not stand around him.

In the seventeenth century AD, Sir Isaac Newton made white light pass through prisms and formulated the laws of reflection and refraction. He showed that white light is made up of seven colours as in the rainbow. These colours had varied wavelengths and were named VIBGYOR = Violet, Indigo, Blue, Green, Yellow, Orange, and Red. The auras are seen to have these seven basic colours, and some more. These seven colours are basically associated with the seven *chakras* in the human body. Clear and shining colours mean that the associated chakra is well developed, while dull and muddy colours mean undeveloped or sick chakras.

In 1908, Dr Walter J. Kilner made an important discovery by which people could see the auras. He divided auras into three parts:

- A narrow and transparent dark space called etheric double.
- The nearly constant and densest portion called inner aura.
- The inconstant portion that blended into the inner aura, called outer aura.

Kilner said that aura reflected the state of health and he formulated a method of auric diagnosis of illness by 1919. Oscar Begnall, who developed a screen which could also be worn as eyeglasses called aura-goggles, continued Kilner's work. Around the same time, C.W. Leadbeater published his remarkable work about seeing men clairvoyantly.

In the early 1940s, Russian electrician and inventor, Semyon Kirlian developed a technique for photographing the biofields or auras. His work was brought to the West in the 1960s. Health and emotions are revealed in Kirlian photos by changes in the brightness, colours and patterns of light in auras. Thelma Moss and Kendall

Johnson of University of California at Los Angeles observed changes in a plant's glow as the human hand approached it and pricked it. A team of scientists including Moss and Kendall further observed similar changes in humans' glow with changes in their emotional states. Photographs of psychic Uri Geller from Tel Aviv and of other psychics revealed flares of light emanating from their fingertips when engaged in their work. Some experiments reporting diagnosis of cancer through Kirlian photography have been successful. Energy or colour fields were always seen around plants, animals, and persons by famous mediums such as Edgar Cayce and Eileen J. Garrett. In the 1950s, Dr Mikhail Kuzmich Gaikin and Vladislav Mikalevsky of Russia developed an electronic device, which could pinpoint nearly 700 Chinese acupuncture points through aura photographs.

As observed by Elizabeth Fuller (1989), medical science now recognises aura as a thin pulsating field around the human body. According to clairvoyants, health and emotions are shown through different colours, energy patterns and breaks, and through clear and muddy spots in the aura. Healers have observed that illness manifests first in the etheric body, which is closest to the physical body, several days, months or even years before the appearance of physical symptoms in the body.

Defining the Aura

All animate and inanimate matter has an atomic structure in which electrons and protons are in constant motion. This motion creates an energy field which has electrical and magnetic vibrations. This energy field around the body is called 'aura'. Aura is therefore such an integral part of the body that it should be taken as an extension of the body. Because the atoms of animate life are more active and vibrant, the auras of living things are more pronounced than those of inanimate things.

Most of us experience aura in our daily life, whether we know about it or not. For example, you instantly like or dislike a person, depending on whether your auric vibrations match or does not match with that of the other person. This explains the theory of 'love at first sight', which occurs because the chemistry of two persons is identical; it may not necessarily mean that the two persons have been acquaintances in previous lives. It may or may not be so. Similarly, you feel more comfortable with certain smells, sounds and colours, according to aura matching. Certain other smells, sounds and colours are unbearable to you since their auric vibrations are exactly opposite to those of yours. In the company of some people you feel energised, while being around certain other people you feel drained. You sometimes feel it, when someone is staring at you. On entering certain rooms you like to stay there, while other rooms offend you in some way and make you angry.

The existence of aura is a fact accepted by science today. Scientists agree that there is a physical field around us, which has infrared energy, electrostatic and electromagnetic radiation. Although opinions of people do not always agree, the existence of colours and consciousness in an aura is now commonly acknowledged by people of all beliefs. The more healthy and spiritual you are, the larger and clearer would be your aura. The stronger the aura, the greater the defence against outside forces. The weaker the aura, the greater the chances of getting tired soon and being manipulated by others.

Just as Newton discovered seven colours hidden in white light, clairvoyants and psychics see these seven basic colours and many others in the aura. A complete analysis of physical, mental, emotional and spiritual personalities is possible through the observation and analysis of colours in an aura, just as is done in numerology. The aura even contains the history of the past and predictions for the future. Auras are not created by light, but light is required to see them. Auras get larger in sunlight and smaller in dim light.

Anyone can see the aura and its colours with sustained practice and patience. In fact, we all have some psychic powers as children, which slowly fade away as we grow wiser in the ways of the world. Emotional attachment sometimes triggers the sight of an aura. Some people have reported seeing the aura of a loved one, because they care intensely about his/her welfare, while some have reported seeing the aura of a weak and tired person in a room with many people in it, though the auras of others were not visible to him/her. It seems that the auras grow and get enlarged in intense situations.

The human aura surrounds the physical body nearly in the shape of an egg, and it has energies of two kinds: physical and subtle. Physical energies from the body are comprised of electrical, magnetic, heat, light, sound and electro-magnetic fields, and these fields are measurable. Subtle energies come from six subtle bodies we possess, forming six layers around the physical body (which is the seventh). Each layer corresponds to a specific function in life. The seven divisions also correspond to the seven chakras or energy vortices in the body (see the following table and Figure 2).

Chakra	Subtle layer	Function
Sahasrara (Crown)	Divine	Unmanifested
Ajna (Brow)	Monadic	Manifested
Vishuddhi (Throat)	Atmic	Spiritual
Anahata (Heart)	Intuitional	Love
Manipura (Solar)	Mental	Thought/Intellect
Swadhishthan (Sacral)	Astral	Sentiments
Mooladhara (Root)	Physical	Karma

Table of Subtle Layers in Aura, and their Function

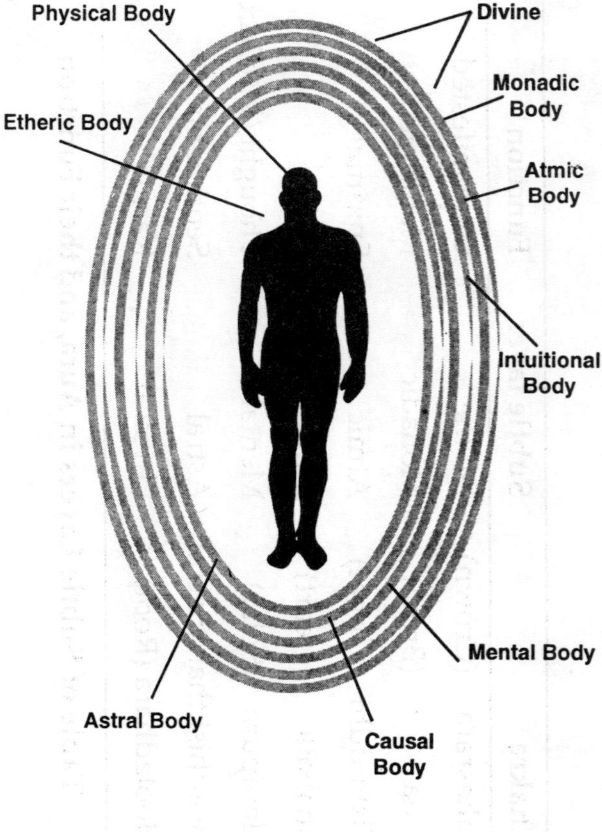
Physical Body
Divine
Monadic Body
Etheric Body
Atmic Body
Intuitional Body
Mental Body
Astral Body
Causal Body

Figure 2

An aura is usually in the shape of an egg surrounding the body, and its size is directly proportional to the spiritual development of the person. It is believed that the aura of Buddha extended to several miles. This is the reason why a large number of people were attracted to him. The aura of an average person extends to several feet. A person indulging in unlawful activities or a miser, for example, will have a small aura with murky colours. Each subtle body governs a particular aspect of the person. Thus, astral aura governs the sentiments or emotions of the person; mental aura takes care of the thought process and intellect; intuitional aura is responsible for love and inner knowledge; *atmic* aura governs spirituality; and monadic and divine auras govern the manifested and unmanifested aspects of God – Absolute, respectively. All of them simultaneously affect the last sheath, that is, the physical body, and what we see in a person is the combined effect of all the subtle bodies. Conversely, one can read every sheath of the aura and know about every aspect of the person.

Normally the energies flow in vertical and horizontal directions. Some waves flow from the spinal column and head towards the boundaries, and the result is an interwoven mesh.

Etheric body/double is a grey matter immediately surrounding the body in a thickness of up to half an inch (see Figure 3). Health and emotional variations first affect the etheric body, and these can be known through variations in colours, energy patterns and brightness/dullness, etc. Some standard symbols are sometimes

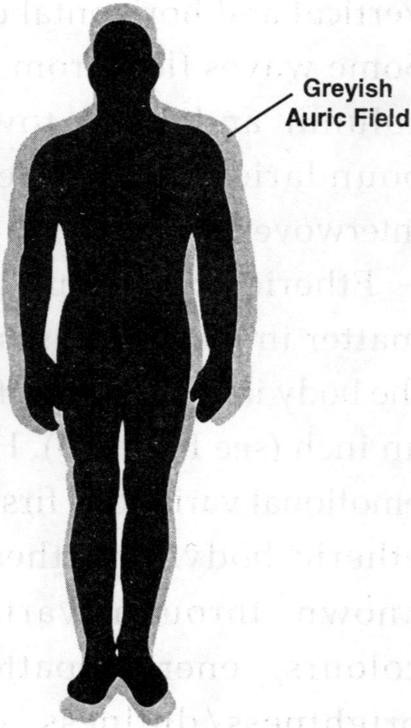

Figure 3
Etheric Body

seen in an aura, for example, a circle denoting wholeness, a triangle denoting protection, a cross denoting indecision, a star denoting paranormal faculty, an arrow denoting stress and strain, etc.

Every person has a unique frequency and every aura is unique in this way. Of course, there are similarities and dissimilarities. Similar auras attract each other and get combined, while dissimilar auras repel each other (see Figures 4 and 5). This is why you like or dislike a person at first sight. However, opposite auras may begin

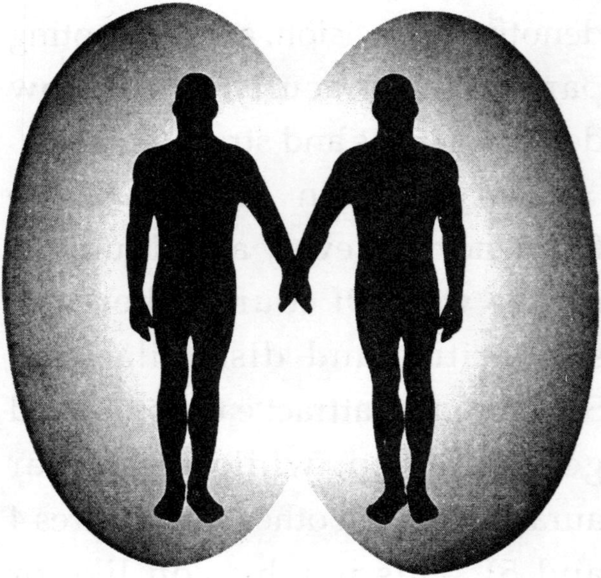

Figure 4
Auras Combine

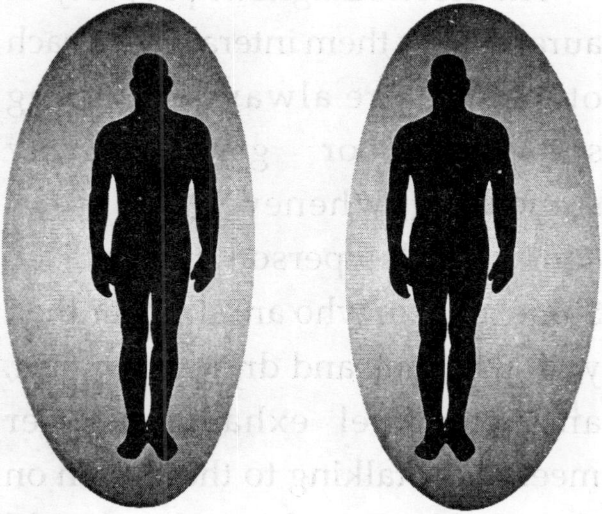

Figure 5
Auras Repel

to like each other as a result of concerted and patient efforts.

The electromagnetic property of auras makes them interact with each other. You are always absorbing something or giving away something, whenever you are in contact with a person or an object. Some of them who are stronger than you, will suck and drain your aura, and you feel exhausted after meeting or talking to them even on the phone. For this, you should make your aura stronger by physical exercises, deep breathing, spiritual practices, etc. Yogis are strong enough not to be affected by any evil. It is good to be around animals, plants and nature at regular intervals, since you absorb energy from them. Hugging a tree is a healthy habit. Crystals and suitable stones also make your aura strong. Totems have a similar, though limited, effect on humans.

Energy exchange is directly proportional to the length and intimacy of the contact. Objects, persons, rooms, etc., get charged with your energy, and this charging is deeper and nearly permanent if the contact is repeated and sustained for longer periods. Toys of children, beds we sleep on, rooms we live in, shawls and blankets of meditating yogis, our regular sex partner—they all get charged with our energy, and we feel comfortable being with them whenever we are exhausted; they recharge our batteries. It is easy to get concentration and *samadhi* on the same cushion and same room, since they have been used for a long time.

Generous and kind persons have large auras with radiant and luminous colours. They spend their lives helping others quietly, many times unnoticed by others, many times taken for granted by friends and relatives, but the nature or psyche, which has the records of everyone's doings like a bank, recognises them. Two people in love have most attractive auras, with colours dancing in them, the two merging in one and the single aura getting enlarged, touching the heights of spirituality. Self-centred and highly materialistic people have small auras with dull and muddy colours. However, the appearance and intensity of colours keep changing throughout the day according to the current situation in life.

Feeling the Aura

Dependence on doctors has reduced our innate power and control, and our recognition of other subtle energies. There are exercises designed to increase our awareness and perception of subtle energies, which had closed down in childhood and are dormant at present. Practice and persistence can enable us to know others and ourselves more intimately. We should first develop a 'relaxed concentration' by meditation, slow and deep breathing, and by moving our awareness from feet upwards to the crown centre. Visualise every part of the body in this journey. Some soothing music can be of assistance. The better the relaxation, the better the concentration, and higher the sensitivity. You will begin to feel that smells are now stronger, colours are brighter, sounds are louder, and so on. In other words, perception abilities have been amplified.

Rub the palms of both hands together for about half-a-minute. Extend the hands in front of you up to one-and-a-half feet, separating them by about two feet, palms facing each other. Move the hands towards each other, as close as possible, without touching them. Now draw them away from each other to a distance of about six inches. Bring them close again and repeat the movement in slow motion for some time (see Figure 6). Be aware of the experience – it could be heating, cooling, tickling, pressurising a rubber ball, pulsating, or a thickness building between the two hands. Note your experience carefully because it is

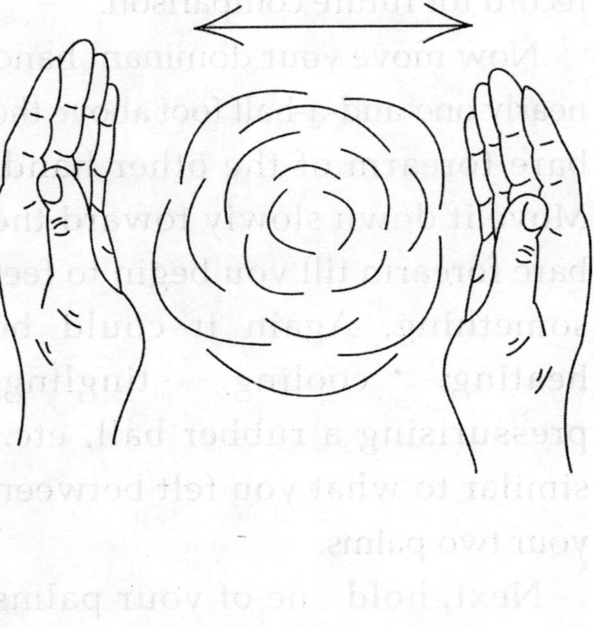

Figure 6

unique. It may or may not be different from the experience of someone else. It is good to keep a record for future comparison.

Now move your dominant hand nearly one-and-a-half foot above the bare forearm of the other hand. Move it down slowly toward the bare forearm till you begin to feel something. Again it could be heating, cooling, tingling, pressurising a rubber ball, etc., similar to what you felt between your two palms.

Next, hold one of your palms facing upward and point the index finger of the other hand towards the palm of the first hand. The distance may be up to six inches. Now gather some energy by slow and deep breathing for a while. Then rotate the index finger in small circles, and create a vortex of energy imagining that you are touching the open palm. Eyes may be closed or open (see Figure 7). The greater the mental projection, the stronger the sensation. Become aware of the feeling as before and make a note of it. A variation can be made by projecting the mental energy vortex on a bare forearm as before, or on

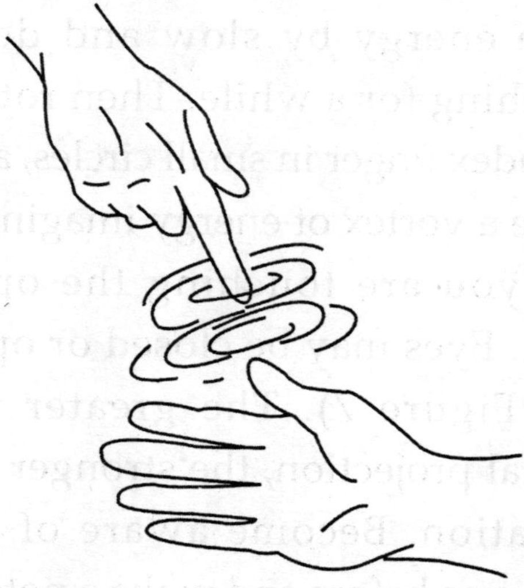

Figure 7

the back of another person. You can move your index finger in the form of small circles, squares or triangles and let the other person detect what geometrical figure you are making on his or her back, without touching.

The distance should gradually be increased in all experiments to find out how far you can go to bring the desired results. All this is about increasing your awareness and perception of subtle energy fields, and to prove to you that thought can create energy.

'Radiesthesia devices' such as dowsing rods or pendulums can measure the size of the aura. These devices are a practical way of communicating with the subconscious mind. Dowsing rods are a pair of L-shaped pieces of metal (Figure 8), the longer side being ten to twelve inches long, and the shorter side about six inches long. One can easily make a set from two wire coat hangers. The shorter sections can be placed inside two plastic straws, or straws made by rolling cardboard and taping it, so that the rods can move freely. One can also use one's loosely held fists, but a tendency to grip the rods

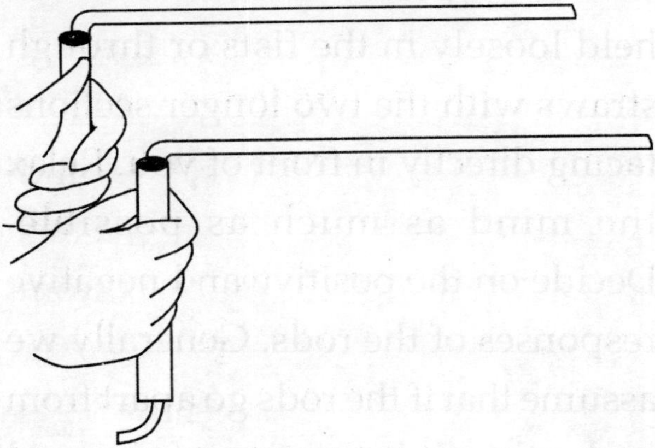

Figure 8
Dowsing Rods

firmly, consciously or unconsciously, obstructs the free movement of rods.

The angle rods should now be held loosely in the fists or through straws with the two longer sections facing directly in front of you. Relax the mind as much as possible. Decide on the positive and negative responses of the rods. Generally we assume that if the rods go apart from each other, it is the sign of yes, and their crossing each other is the sign of no. But we have to tell this to the rods before starting the experiments. If we do not say anything to the rods, then any response, called dowsing, will indicate the outer boundary of the aura. Ask the person under experiment to stand with his/her legs and arms slightly spread. Stand about 30 feet away from the person holding the two rods in front of you. Move forward slowly until the rods begin to respond. Take a pause and move forward more slowly until the rods either cross over or move apart from each other (see Figure 9). This is the outer edge of the person's aura. Note the distance from the person, and with this as radius, you

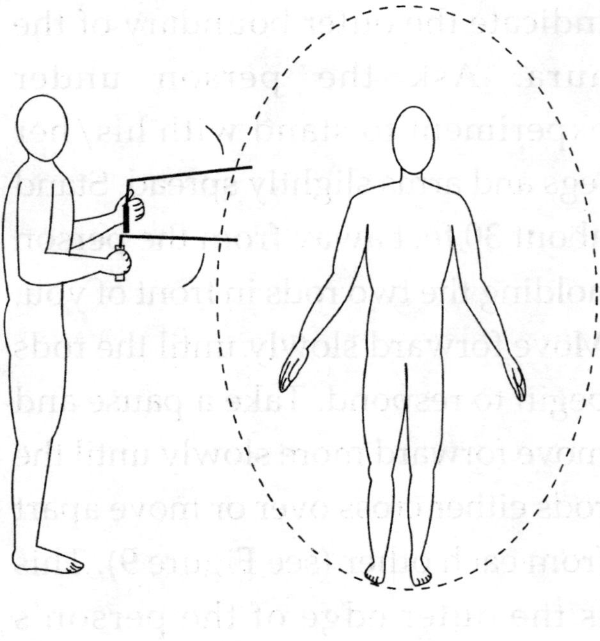

Figure 9
Measuring your Auric Field

can draw a circle around him to indicate the field of aura. The same radius will be found when experimenting from any direction. The aura may appear very large, but it is the inner layers which you feel, when it comes to feeling the aura. A comparison of the radii will classify people according to their spiritual evolution.

Our conscious mind is normally only aware of that upon which it is focused, that is, organised brain activity, and that which can be experienced through the five senses of touch, sight, smell, sound and taste. The subconscious mind is aware of energy interactions from both sources – the five physical senses and beyond. All these interactions can be brought into the conscious through relaxation methods, such as hypnosis, meditation, radiesthesia, etc. Organised brain activities radiate beta waves and control only ten per cent of the body and brain activities. Relaxation methods radiate alpha-wave patterns, and control about 90 per cent of the body and brain activities. The autonomic nervous system, which regulates the sensitive organs of our body, is directed by the subconscious. Interactions of outside agencies with our auric field are transmitted through our skin to our body and brain. A pendulum acts as a bridge between our subconscious and conscious minds. It is an amplifier. The subconscious mind, through the sympathetic nervous system, stimulates involuntary muscle action and thus causes the pendulum to move. However, we must learn to keep our emotions out, for this translation to take place (see Figure 10). You can buy a

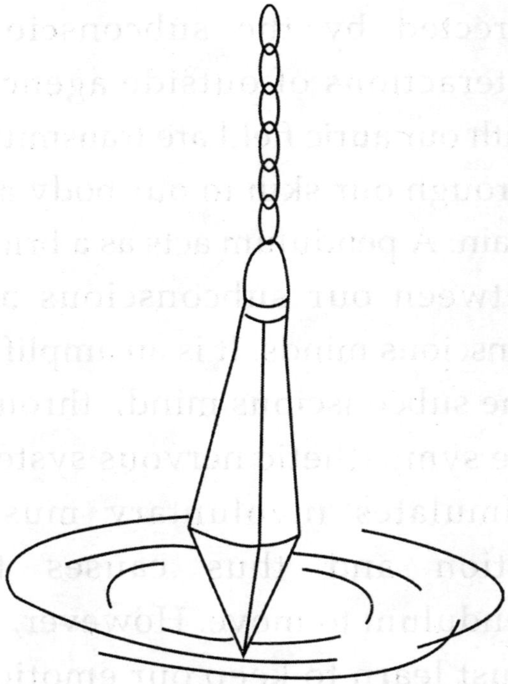

Figure 10
A Quartz Pendulum

pendulum from a shop or make one of your own. It is good to use a crystal since it has greater sensitivity to subtle forces, but any object such as a ring, a button, a cork, etc., can be used.

Programming the Pendulum

Relax yourself by any method. Take up position at a table with your elbows resting on it. Hold the pendulum with your thumb and index finger. To familiarise yourself with it, give it vertical, horizontal, clockwise, and anticlockwise motions, giving it a rest after each type of motion. Now ask the pendulum to "move clockwise" through your power of thought, visualising that the power is passing from your body to the chain to the pendulum. No physical power should be used. When it starts swinging for a while, you can ask it mentally to "stop", and see that it stops completely. Now you can programme it the way you want. You may ask it to swing clockwise if the answer to a question is "yes", and anticlockwise if the answer is "no". Or, you may ask it to have a vertical motion for a 'yes' and a horizontal motion for a 'no', or any other set of directions you may choose for the purpose. You may talk loudly to your subconscious to give these particular motions to the pendulum in answer to a question.

Asking Questions

For verification now, you may ask some simple questions, such as, saying your name correctly and asking the pendulum whether it is right or wrong. See that the pendulum moves in the direction fixed for a 'yes'. Now say an incorrect name and check if the answer of the pendulum is negative. You may speak your right age and see if the pendulum confirms it with a "yes". Then speak the wrong age and see if it says "no". Ask the pendulum, "Am I a vegetarian?" and check if it answers you correctly. You may ask, "Is Monica my friend?" and verify that it gives the correct answer. Now you are ready to ask questions whose answers are not known to you. For example, you may ask, "Am I going to travel abroad next month?" If it says "no", you may increase the time and keep on asking till it says "yes", which should be the time you may actually make a journey abroad. You may ask, "Am I going to get a promotion in a fortnight? Am I going to incarnate again? Will I see my friend John next week? Is John in good health?" The accuracy of the answers will be directly proportional to the extent you keep emotions away from the experiment.

Measurement of Aura

Measurement of aura with a pendulum can be carried out in two ways. One way is through questions. You may ask the pendulum if your aura is between 15 and 20 feet. If not, ask if it is between 12 and 15 feet. Go on till the answer is "yes". Then reduce the period of variation or ask straight away if it is 10 feet, and so on. You will know the size of the aura to a fairly precise extent.

Another way is the direct method of holding the pendulum at the root and asking it to tell the size of the aura of the person under experiment. Relax, give instructions to your subconscious and the pendulum, and then walk slowly towards the person. It is better to programme it to give a circular motion on reaching the outer edge of the aura, since a horizontal or vertical motion can be mistaken because of the disturbance caused by your walking. Walk and pause, walk again and pause. The moment you get a circular motion, it is an indication that you have reached the outer edge of the aura (see Figure 11). However, the dowsing method of rods is easier and quicker for this purpose.

The chakras can be easily located through feeling, and their intensity can be measured approximately through the pendulum. The seven chakras lie on the spine at the following positions in the body:

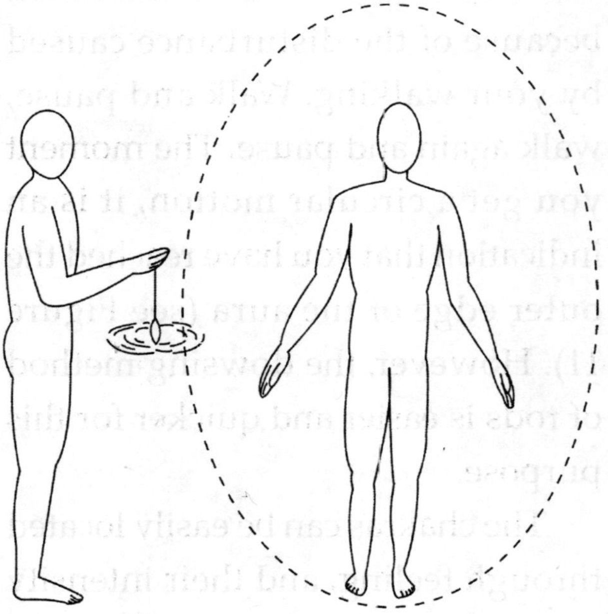

Figure 11
Measuring the Aura with a Pendulum

1.	Root	Mid-point between the anus and the genitals
2.	Sacral	One inch inside at the level of the end of the tailbone
3.	Solar	Behind the navel
4.	Heart	Centre of the chest at the level of the heart
5.	Throat	Behind the throat pit
6.	Eyebrow	At the intersection of the horizontal (through the centre of the eyebrows) and the vertical (through the centre of the head).
7.	Crown	Top of the head

You can feel the high order of energy emanated by the chakras when compared to any other part of the body, except of course, the fingers and toes. It would be a surprisingly pleasant experience. You can place one (or both) hands in front of the root centre at a distance of about one foot. Bring it slowly towards the root centre till you feel some resistance. Pull it away a little and then move it forward again. Finally you reach a point, which is the definite boundary of the aura. If the same experiment is performed at a point near the root chakra (not exactly at the chakra), you can bring your hand closer to the body without resistance, than in the former case. This explains the higher energy at the chakras. After locating the root chakra, locate all the higher chakras one by one in the same manner (see Figure 12).

To increase your awareness of the chakras, you can ask your friend to lie down and you can locate all his/her chakras. Your friend can do the same for you. Each one of you should pay attention to the point when the other person touches the boundary of the aura. You can feel the intrusion of your auric field by the other person consciously. You

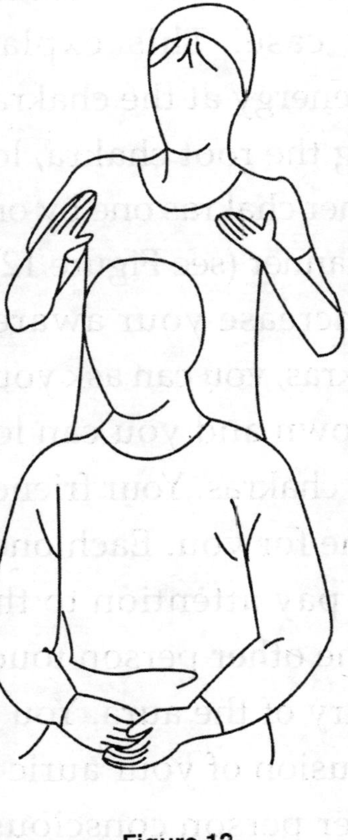

Figure 12
Feeling the Aura

can experiment in a similar manner by facing the corner of a room, and asking your friend to move towards you slowly from the other corner. The moment he/she enters your auric field, you should be able to feel it. Interchange positions with your friend and see if he/she also feels your intrusion into his/her auric field. Such an auric field is called 'personal space' or 'psychological aura'.

Now you can use a pendulum and programme it to oscillate clockwise if a chakra is open. Also instruct your subconscious and the pendulum to oscillate with a speed proportional to the opening of the chakra. Thus, if a chakra is closed, the pendulum will not move at all. On the other extreme, if it is fully open, the pendulum will oscillate very rapidly, making large circles. Now ask your friend to lie down on his/her back so that you can hang the pendulum on each chakra one by one (see Figure 13). Note the movement of the pendulum at each chakra, which tells you the degree to which each chakra is open.

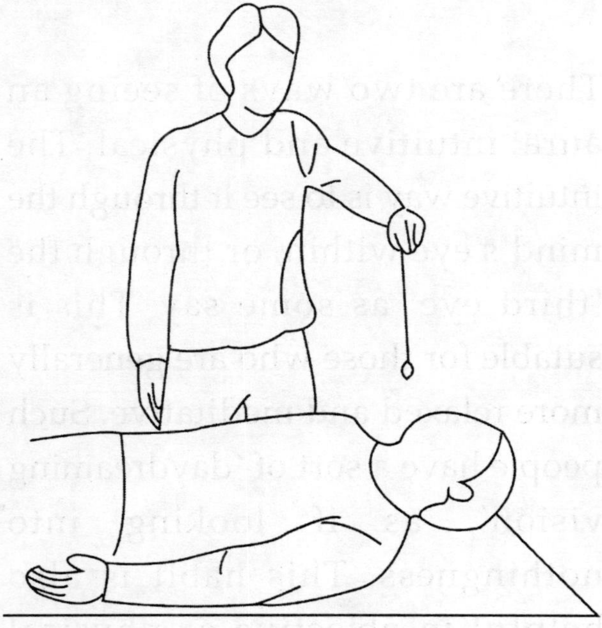

Figure 13
Feeling the Aura with a Pendulum

Seeing the Aura

There are two ways of seeing an aura: intuitive and physical. The intuitive way is to see it through the mind's eye within, or through the 'third eye' as some say. This is sutable for those who are generally more relaxed and meditative. Such people have a sort of 'daydreaming vision', as if looking into nothingness. This habit is also helpful in objective or physical visualisation of the aura with practice and persistence. Although both methods carry equal importance, the physical or objective viewing of aura carries the advantage of greater tangibility of subtle energies, such as the one possessed by dowsing rods and the pendulum.

Seeing the aura physically is a natural ability with almost everyone. It is normally more pronounced in childhood, but the elders in the house never encourage children to devote time to it for several reasons. This ability is thus seemingly lost and remains dormant, until evoked through special practices.

Ways of Seeing the Aura

Perform some relaxation exercises, such as meditation, and soft deep breathing, for some time. Begin with experimentation in a relaxed mood; a result-oriented, rigid view may deter success for some time. Tell yourself that it does not matter if you do not see anything today. It is good to begin with seeing one of your hands with the palm facing towards you, at a distance of one to one-and-a half feet, against a white background, in a dimly lit room. Some people prefer a black background for the visibility of auric lights. Keep a soft focus on the finger tips and around, like the daydreaming vision of nothingness. Sooner or later, today or tomorrow, you will begin to see a soft haze around your fingers. With continued practice, colours will begin to appear as dots or flashes in the beginning.

Alternate between concentration and soft focusing on the hand for about half-a-minute each. The haze will begin to appear around the fingers and hands with continued practice for a few days; only in some cases it might take a month or so. Be aware of the dots or flashes of colours which may appear in the aura from time to time; do not dismiss them as fantasy or something else. Slowly you will be able to hold the colours (see Figure 14).

Now hold both hands, 3 to 4 inches apart, palms facing towards you, at the level of your eyes. Concentrate on the edges or on the space between the fingers for about half-a-minute and then shift the focus to the area surrounding the two hands. Keep looking at the outline of the hands against the

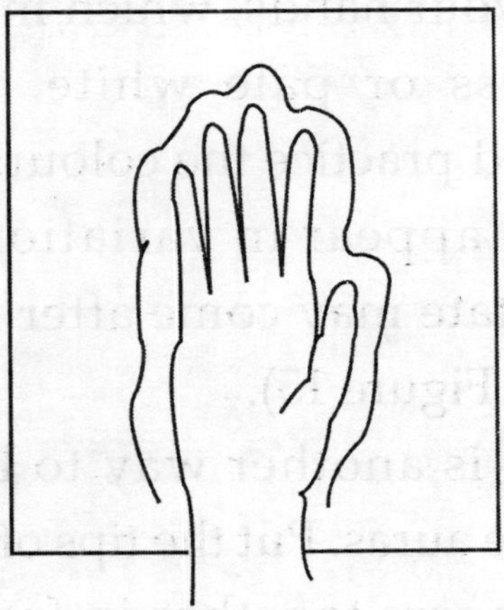

Figure 14
Aura about One Hand

white background. Although the experiences vary from person to person, you normally see a soft haze around your hands, which may be colourless or pale white. With continued practice the colours will begin to appear in variations. A steady state may come after some time (see Figure 15).

There is another way to begin seeing the auras. Put the tips of your index fingers together in front of you, for about 15 seconds. Then slowly pull them apart. You may see a fine thread of energy between them, which may disappear as the

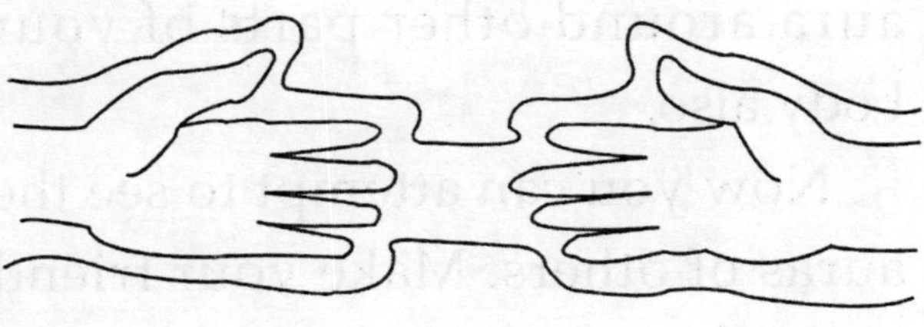

Figure 15
Aura about Two Hands

distance becomes more than half-an-inch in the beginning. Gradually you may use all the fingers of your hands, or at times one or more fingers with your partner (see Figure 16). You may start to see the aura around other parts of your body also.

Now you can attempt to see the auras of others. Make your friend stand about ten feet away from you against a white (or black) wall, in a dimly lit room. Look at the forehead of your friend for a while, and then move your eyes in a clockwise direction around his/her whole

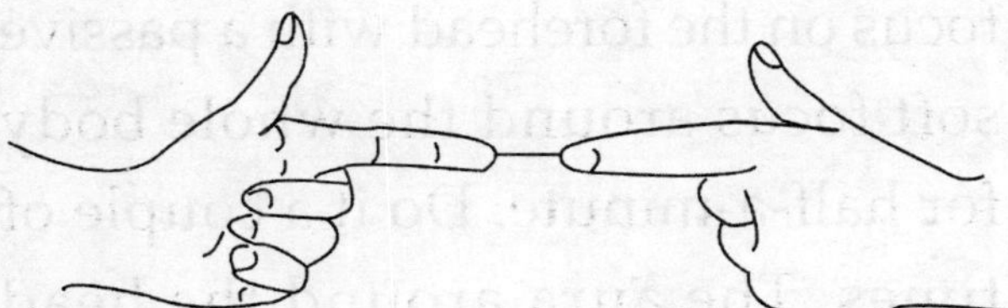

Figure 16

body. The movement of the eyes should be quick so that the powers of the eyes are evoked. Coming back to the forehead, keep your eyes focused on it for about half-a-minute. Alternate the concentrated focus on the forehead with a passive soft focus around the whole body for half-a-minute. Do it a couple of times. The aura around the head may appear first, and it is more pronounced than that around any other part of the body (see Figure 17). A hazy aura may appear around the whole body, like the one you saw around your own hand in the

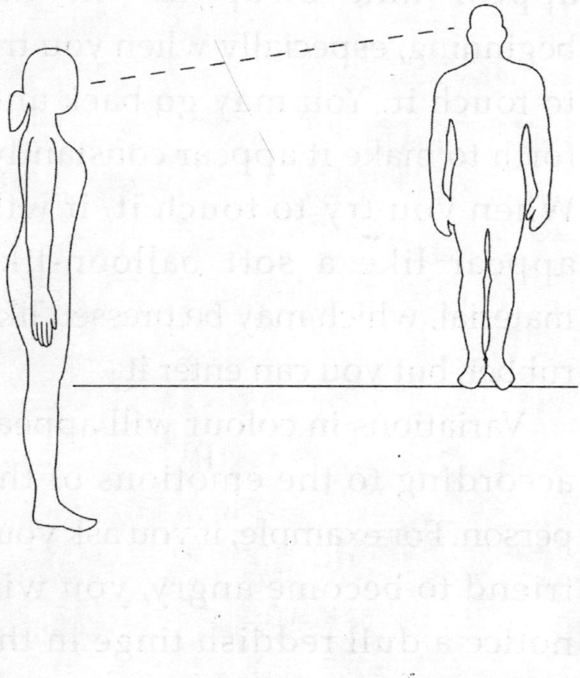

Figure 17
Looking at the Auras of Others

beginning. Remember that clothing obstructs the aura. The aura may appear and disappear in the beginning, especially when you try to touch it. You may go back and forth to make it appear constantly. When you try to touch it, it will appear like a soft balloon-like material, which may be pressed like rubber, but you can enter it.

Variations in colour will appear according to the emotions of the person. For example, if you ask your friend to become angry, you will notice a dull reddish tinge in the aura. If he/she becomes happy and cheerful, either by remembering something nice or by deep breathing, you can see that the aura becomes larger. You can also observe that the parts of aura around the chakras move rapidly in circular motions. You can practise seeing the aura of your friend when he/she is walking in a crowded area. You can also try to observe the auras of other people in the crowd. However, it should be remembered that you see auras best when there is dim light and a clear white or black background. Early mornings and late afternoons are the best times.

Colours of the Aura — Life Reading

Very often we hear statements such as, "He was red with anger", "It was a golden opportunity for you", "She was green with envy", "You are in a black mood" or "She was feeling blue". These statements must have appeared long after people observed a relation between moods or sentiments and colours.

You must have observed that in places of entertainment and fairs, etc., the yellow colour is dominant, since it is the colour of 'self-expression' and 'joy of life', represented by the number '3' in numerology. You might have noticed that the hats of kings, queens, priests, etc., are predominantly violet in colour since it is the colour of peace, tranquillity, aloofness and spirituality, represented by the number '7' in numerology. Scientists have discovered that prisoners get excited and become aggressive when they are exposed to red light, and they calm down under a blue light or a pink light. Red relates to the number '1' and represents leadership and aggression. Blue relates to the number '5' and represents knowledge and constructive freedom. Pink relates to the number '8' and represents administration and materialism.

Green corresponds to the heart chakra and represents compassion and healing. Restaurateurs are beginning to use orange and red colours, since orange stimulates appetite and red makes the time move faster, so that more customers can be served in the same time. Orange is the colour of sacral chakra and red is the colour of root chakra.

The preceding paragraphs are enough to show the importance of colours in our life, whether we take advantage of this knowledge or not. Moreover, colours are related to chakras and numbers, which will be elaborated later.

Colours closest to the physical body represent physical energy and health. Colours in the outer regions represent mental, emotional and spiritual energies. Clear and bright colours represent good conditions and a fulfilled person. Dull, muddy and thick colours represent overactivity, imbalances and problems. Colours in auras change frequently according to changes in physical, mental, emotional and spiritual conditions. However, the aura has a certain colour or colours which are permanent and primary, while others are secondary. The primary/permanent colour represents the purpose of life in this incarnation; it corresponds to the 'talent number' calculated through the 'date of birth' of the person in numerology. Secondary colours represent prevailing conditions at the moment. Hence, caution should be exercised in interpreting colours.

Meaning of Colours

The aura contains the seven colours that make up white light or sunlight or the rainbow – VIBGYOR (violet, indigo, blue, green, yellow, orange, and red), and also colours outside the rainbow. The meaning of colours and related numbers are given below in brief.

Number 1 – Red

Independent, courageous, individualised, original, creative and inventive, possessing leadership qualities and executive ability, strong-willed, determined, action-oriented. The colour may appear dull and weak in childhood, but it improves with age. If red is the primary colour, the person is likely to acquire leadership qualities and a prominent position in life.

Negative effect

Aggressive, boastful, self-centred, dominating, egotistic.

Number 2-Orange

Cooperative, peaceful, diplomatic, adaptable, modest, friendly, gracious, meditative, spiritual. When orange is the primary colour, the person is likely to be diplomatic, tactful and intuitive. He/she might end up being a missionary or peacemaker.

Negative effect
Shy, timid, effeminate, unhappy, lonely.

Number 3 — Yellow
Self-expressive, joyous, artistic and creative, imaginative, inspirational, possessing the gift of words, versatile, optimistic, happy, brilliant, prophetic, cheerful and merry. When yellow is the primary colour, people are likely to be crowned with success in creative ventures, provided they are true to their purpose.

Negative effect
Scattered forces, extravagant, prone to loose talk and exaggeration, self-centred.

Number 4 – Green
Constructive, systematic, orderly, practical, down-to-earth, steady, calm, efficient, serious, responsible, industrious, honest, faithful, determined. When green is the primary colour, people tend to care for others with a motherly attitude, and can end up being healers in any form.

Negative effect

Fixed ideas, argumentative, extremely serious and dominating.

Number 5 – Blue

Versatile, resourceful, active, loving freedom and change, entertaining and amusing, sensuous, quick in thinking, clever. When blue is the primary colour, it makes the person feel young at heart, and successful in public relations work.

Negative effect

Having many irons in the fire, they may remain 'jack of all trades and master of none' – restless, nervous, discontented, loving change and variety, and lustful.

Number 6 – Indigo

Balanced, responsible, artistic, creative, loyal, dependable, unselfish, harmonious, just, righteous, domesticated, generous. When indigo is the primary colour, people tend to have a worthwhile humanitarian type of occupation.

Negative effect

They find it difficult to say 'no' to others and are taken advantage of by people. Too much love of duty, involvement in troubles of others, self-sacrifice and family ties can make their life barren and lonely.

Number 7 – Violet

Analytical, understanding, intellectual, observant, inventive; loving solitude, philosophy, meditation, mysticism and the occult. They are perfectionists with a dignified, charming personality. When violet is the primary colour, people are seen developing spiritually all the way, and may end up teaching Higher Laws.

Negative effect

Too much reservedness, inadaptability and lack of trust in others can make them aloof, confused and depressed. Pride, hidden motives and over-positiveness can lead them into wrong situations.

Number 8 – Pink

Materialistic, tough, tenacious, authoritative, efficient, organised, judgemental, capable of working for a cause, competent in management and administration, ambitious, dependable. When pink is the primary colour, people are found to be stubborn and they are likely to achieve power and positions of authority and acquire material possessions.

Negative effect

Over ambitiousness and too much materialism can lead to strain and tension and sometimes a breakdown. Jealousy can mar their personal lives. Love of recognition, display of powers, lack of humanitarianism and consideration for others are other negative qualities. They are obstinate and impatient.

Number 9 – Bronze

Selfless, humanitarian, forgiving, compassionate, tolerant, generous, broadminded, charitable, philanthropic, religious, artistic and dramatic, impulsive, unorthodox, spiritual and capable of living divine standards of life. When bronze is the primary colour, people are seen working for philanthropic and humanitarian projects for the welfare of others. They are capable of achieving spiritual heights, if they are true to their purpose.

Negative effects

Moody, impulsive, changeable in love affairs, careless in money matters. High living can bring health and other problems.

Number 11 — Silver

Humanitarian, intuitive, prophetic. People with silver as their primary colour are full of great ideas but more often than not, impractical. However, if they live to the purpose rightly, they will end up being enlightened, possessing cosmic consciousness. Sometimes there are soft twinkling lights, which are important indicators of significant creativity and fertility. In many cases they indicate pregnancy for women, but in general they may signify the opening of a new door in the person's life. They mean that you are involved in useful creative activities.

Negative effect

Hypersensitive, nervous, impractical and selfish. I have seen many of them suffering from broken relationships, perhaps due to karmic destiny, carrying the debris from a past life.

Number 22 — Gold

Master builder, mastermind, very capable, wise, creative, spiritual, luminary. People with gold as their primary colour possess the ability to handle large-scale projects with ease, and may achieve anything they have in mind as a goal. If they live rightly to the purpose, they are sure to be crowned with success and be known as VIPs in their field of interest.

Negative effect

It is difficult for them to get over the conflict between inner feelings and practicality, or, in other words, to express spirituality in a practical way. I have seen them taking on more work than they can handle, and being unable to complete the project, they cut a sorry figure in the end. Jealousy, malevolence and attraction for black magic are some of the negative aspects.

Remarks

7 (violet colour) and 22 (gold colour) are both spiritual in nature. In mathematics they are related through the Greek letter 'pi' which equals 22/7, giving the ratio of the circumference of the circle to its diameter. The Hebrew language contains 22 alphabets and was said to be the language of God.

The colours discussed above are basic colours, and they have a relation to numbers as shown above. There are some other colours, which have the following meanings:

White

White is the composite of all colours. When white sunlight passes through a prism, it breaks up into the seven colours of the rainbow. And on passing through another prism, the seven colours get combined as white. It is rare to see white as a primary colour. But when it appears, it represents purity, saintly virtues, concern for others, wisdom and intuitive knowledge from beyond. The person appears to be more than his/her years and seems like he has graduated from the school of earth.

Grey

The appearance of silvery grey as the primary colour indicates the awakening of the intuitive faculties leading to illumination. The person should be adept in creative imagination. Dark grey in variations denotes ill health related to specific areas of the body. According to Ted Andrews, grey colour in the aura can indicate a person who is secretive and who is the lone wolf type.

Brown

One should not be hasty in interpreting the brown, which appears quite often in the aura. If close to the body it may mean physical imbalances, around the head it may mean lack of discrimination, and around the chakras it may mean blocked energy and a need for cleansing. However, brown is also the colour of earth and thus it represents new growth and desire for accomplishment, if it appears above the region of the head or below the feet.

Black

Black and dark areas around the physical body may mean a physical imbalance. Black areas around the edge may mean leakage of energy and consciousness from the aura, which may be due to various abuses that one may be accustomed to. Continued abuse that may result in well-formed black holes in the outer skirts, which may not be easy to heal. Only in rare cases, black may imply serious illness or death. It may also mean increasing responsibility for what one does.

Determining the Colours by Other Methods

Our subconscious knows all about the energies, colours, and answers to all questions. We only have to bring the information from the subconscious to the conscious by some method, until we are able to see the auras and colours directly. This can be done in the following two ways:

Numerology

Colours of the aura can be easily found through numbers, which have already been introduced in this section. We now have to know the method of calculating the numbers in the life of a person, so that we can find the corresponding colours and their meanings. For greater details one can refer to my book *Secrets of Numerology* (1992).

The most important number in the life of a person is his/her *talent number* which denotes the purpose of life and lessons to be learnt in life. It is calculated by reducing to a single digit the number of the month, the number of the day and the number of the year of birth, adding them up and again reducing the total to a single digit. For example, a person born on July 22, 1941 will have

Month... July = 7
Day... 22 = 2+2 = 4
Year... 1941= 1+9+4+1 = 15 = 6
Total... = 7+4+6 = 17 = 1+7 = 8

Talent Number 8 = Pink colour

This means that material satisfaction is the main purpose of life. This person will have pink as the primary colour of the aura, when you see it, and will be tough, tenacious, with love of power, position and material possessions.

As another example, take a person born on August 15, 1967

Month... August = 8
Day... 15 = 6
Year... 1967 = 23 = 2+3 = 5
Total... = 8+6+5 = 19 = 1+9 = 10
= 1+0 = 1.

Talent Number 1 = Red colour

This means that individuation, independence and attainment are the tools the person is born with. He/she is likely to do some original work and attain a position of authority, if he/she lives truly to the purpose.

The total should not be reduced to a single digit only when it is either

11 or 22, as these numbers have their own identity.

The other equally important number is the *destiny number*, which is calculated through the name of the person. Destiny number represents the circumstances and opportunities in the life of the person. It has unlimited possibilities, unlike the talent number which has only eleven colours for the eleven numbers in numerology. Following the Pythagorean system, each alphabet is given a number according to the following chart:

1	2	3	4	5	6	7	8	9
A	B	C	D	E	F	G	H	I
J	K	L	M	N	O	P	Q	R
S	T	U	V	W	X	Y	Z	

Let us take the name Ram Prakash, as an example. Giving numerical value to each alphabet in his name we get

RAM

9 1 4 = 9+1+4 = 14 = 1+4 = 5

PRAKASH

7 9 1 2 1 1 8 = 7+9+1+2+1+1+8

=29 = 2+9 = 11 = 1+1 = 2

Total = 5+2 = 7

This is his destiny number which corresponds to the colour violet. If he was born on August 15, 1967, then his talent number '1' represents the colour red. His aura therefore will have red colour as the primary background and violet colour will be predominant around the red.

The next important number is the *heart number* which represents the heart's desire of the person. It is calculated as the sum total of the vowels in his name. In this case we have A+A+A = 1+1+1 = 3, as his heart number, represented by the colour yellow, which should also be found around his primary colour violet.

The life reading of Ram Prakash will thus be as follows: His primary background 'violet' has 'red' and 'yellow' radiating around its outskirts. He is therefore born with a philosophical, philanthropic and spiritual bent of mind and talents. He will find the outlet for his talents through 'red colour', that is, individuation, independence and attainment. Synchronising red with violet now would mean that he will grow spiritually in an independent and individualised manner and will finally attain recognition as a 'spiritual person'. In the later years of his life he is certain to live a saintly life, teaching others about the higher truth as understood by him. His heart's desire is 'yellow' that is, self-expression and joy of living. This means that Ram Prakash will attain recognition as a spiritual person and he will be able to 'express his knowledge successfully to others', and he will have the 'joy of living as a spiritual person.'

Sometimes the position of colours represented by talent, destiny and heart numbers may be interchanged among themselves, according to the way the person is living. It would happen when one is not living true to one's purpose of life, for one reason or the other. Yet, the synchronised result of the colours would be more or less the same. You can advise such people that they are not making right use of their talents and are missing a grand opportunity, which could crown them with success.

There is another important number called *ultimate number*, which represents the ultimate goal of life. This is the total of talent and destiny numbers reduced to a single digit. Thus we have four important numbers—talent, destiny, heart and ultimate—called *major numbers*. Then there are several minor numbers, which relate to the different aspects of life. Reading the past, present and future can be done very effectively through numerology, which is a complete science in itself. Interested readers are referred to my book, *Secrets of Numerology* (1992).

Radiesthesia

The information about colours in the aura can also be found by radiesthetic methods – dowsing and pendulum. Dowsing can be done in two ways: First, by asking questions to the rods, such as, "Is the primary colour of Ram Prakash red?" and then looking for the answer "yes" or "no", according to how the rods are programmed. For example, the two rods that were held parallel before questioning may come together or even overlap each other to mean "yes", or go apart to mean "no". You may talk to the subconscious and the rods before beginning the experiment. If the answer to red is "no", you can next ask about orange, and so on, till the answer is "yes". Then you can ask about the secondary colours one by one and about the location of all these colours. After all the information is collected, you can give a life reading.

Second, you can make a circular chart and colour different sections with all possible colours and also write their names therein. Keeping your feet on the ground and elbows on the table of the chart, hold one rod loosely at the centre of the circle (see Figure 18). Ask the sub-conscious and the rod to move and

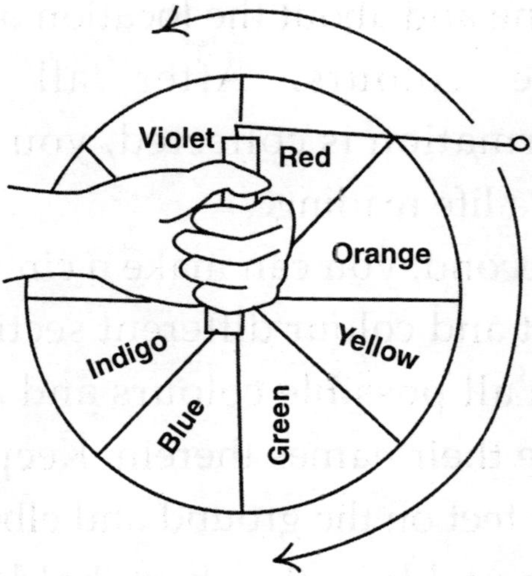

Figure 18
Using the Dowsing Rods to Determine the Colour of the Aura

stop at the division which represents the primary colour of the person under experiment, whether someone else or yourself. Then you can ask the rod to indicate secondary colours one by one, and then the location of all the colours. Now you are ready to give a life reading and even ask further questions, if any.

The pendulum can also be used after programming it to rotate clockwise for 'yes' and anti-clockwise for 'no', or any other possible movements. Make a straight chart showing all possible colours. Move the pendulum on each colour till the answer is "yes" (see Figure 19). All the primary and secondary colours can be determined in this manner, and a life reading can be given.

Colour awareness should be improved so that the colours in the aura can be conveniently detected. There are certain habits and exercises, which can bring improvement in the recognition of colours. You should remain alert in noticing the colours of the dresses you and others wear every day. You may find that everyone has a more or less favourite colour or colours.

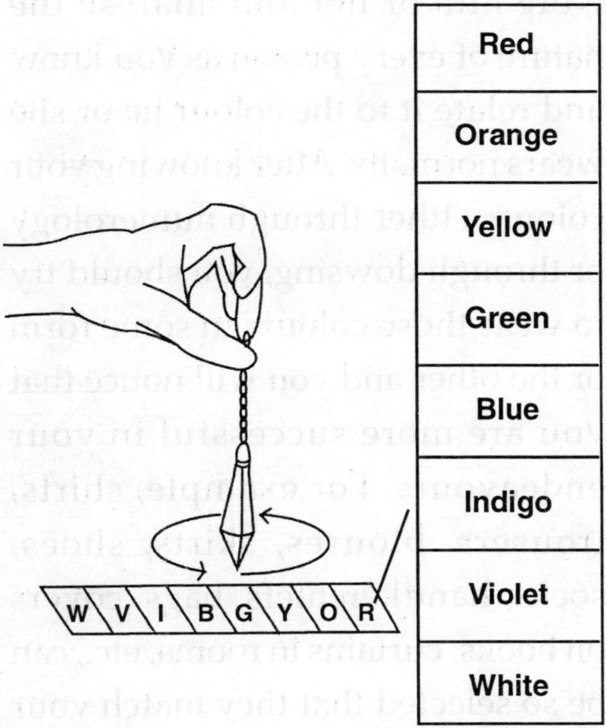

Figure 19
Using the Pendulum to Determine the Colour of the Aura

Note him or her and analyse the nature of every person as you know and relate it to the colour he or she wears normally. After knowing your colours either through numerology or through dowsing, you should try to wear those colours in some form or the other and you will notice that you are more successful in your endeavours. For example, shirts, trousers, blouses, skirts, shoes, socks, handkerchiefs, bags, covers on books, curtains in rooms, etc., can be so selected that they match your primary and secondary colours.

To sharpen your talents, you should wear the colour of your talent number. To be successful in business or daily affairs, you should wear the colour of your destiny number. To see the satisfaction of your heart's desire, you should wear the colour of your heart number as some part of your dress, or at least keep a handkerchief of that colour. To make the force of your ultimate number work in your life, you should wear some part of your dress in that colour. If you are going to meet a particular person and you know his/her colours, you should carry that colour with you in some form or the other, so as to attract the attention of that person and win his/her favour. You can calculate many minor numbers that affect you through numerology, and use related colours to enhance those aspects of life. In any case, it is advisable that major parts of your dress and surroundings are in your primary colour for general success. Make this a habit and see the difference.

Creative imagination is very useful in improving colour awareness. While sitting in a chair comfortably or lying in bed in a relaxed mood, you can close your eyes and inhale deeply the imaginary air of one particular colour. Imagine that that particular colour is pervading your whole body with the breathing and is imparting qualities of that colour/number to you. For example, with red you should imagine that you are becoming individualised, independent and a leader in your field. With orange you should imagine that you are becoming peaceful, cooperative and tactful. And so on. You can use all colours of the rainbow one by one, in the reverse order of VIBGYOR, that is, beginning with red and ending with violet. This can balance your personality with all colours or numbers, and increase the required awareness of colours.

At another time you can imagine that there is a big rainbow in front of you. Enter one colour and get drenched in it completely. Feel that you have become that colour itself and have attained all virtues related to that colour. Move from one end to the other, passing through all colours. Before falling asleep in bed, you can always imagine seeing beautiful surroundings in different colours – meadows, buildings, parks, rivers, mountains or hills, shopping complexes, etc. Your concentration between the eyebrows will increase gradually and this will help in the opening of the 'third eye' or the 'eyebrow chakra'. Unconsciously, you will become more spiritual and philosophical, taking greater interest in the abstract. You may find that you have become more peaceful internally, because of your increased awareness of colours.

Colours in Chakras

Chakras and *Nadis* form a complete subject, which has been dealt with in detail separately in a mini book of this kind. In this book we wish to talk mainly about the colours the chakras have and their effect on human beings (see Figure 20).

The seven chakras are situated in the etheric/causal body along the spinal column of the physical body as shown in Figure 19. They are the vortices of energy, each connected with a specific gland and they can be

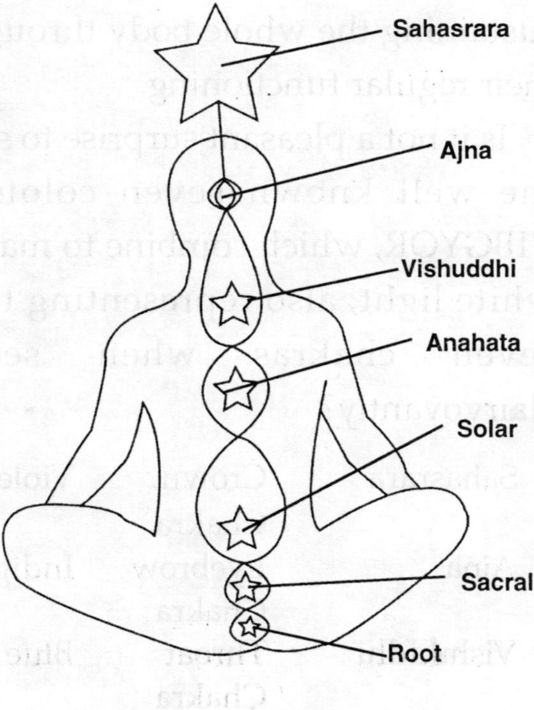

Figure 20
The Chakras

seen by clairvoyants. The chakras are responsible for nourishing and sustaining the whole body through their regular functioning.

Is it not a pleasant surprise to see the well known seven colours VIBGYOR, which combine to make white light, also representing the seven chakras when seen clairvoyantly?

7	Sahasrara	Crown Chakra	Violet
6	Ajna	Eyebrow Chakra	Indigo
5	Vishuddhi	Throat Chakra	Blue
4	Anahata	Heart Chakra	Green

3	Manipura	Solar Chakra	Yellow
2	Swadhishthan	Sacral Chakra	Orange
1	Mooladhara	Root Chakra	Red

A clear and bright primary colour in the aura would indicate a well-developed chakra, while a dull and muddy primary colour would mean an undeveloped chakra. Undeveloped chakras mean negative traits in the personality and an unbalanced aura. The aura can be balanced to a good extent with the aid of the pendulum. It is like taking the negative karma out and throwing it away, unlike the 'guru' taking the negative karma of his disciples on himself. Let us first describe in brief the attributes of chakras.

Mooladhara or Root Chakra

It is situated slightly inside the perineum, near the midpoint between the anus and the scrotum in the males. It lies on the posterior side of the cervix in the females. The vestigial gland called *brahma granthi* lies at the root chakra and blocks the energy. Lord Ganesha (who is known as the remover of obstacles and the source of absolute wisdom) is its presiding deity.

When properly developed, mooladhara represents innocence, chastity, and wisdom. It also governs sex and excretion. If undeveloped it represents adultery, perverted sex, pornography, lustful attention, materialism, constipation and no interest in spirituality. Chakra balancing can take care of these negative aspects to a large extent.

Swadhishthan or Sacral Chakra

It lies at the base of the spine. It can be felt as a bony bulb just above the anus at the level of the tailbone or coccyx. The Sanskrit word *swadhishthan* means 'one's own abode'. It relates to the reproductive and urinary systems and corresponds to the prostate gland in men and utero-vaginal plexus in women. Its presiding deity is Lord Brahma and power is Goddess Saraswati.

When developed, it represents intellectuality, creativity, inspiration, knowledge of beyond and aesthetics. Negatively it means excessive thinking and excessive involvement in artistic things, ego-oriented life, overindulgence in alcohol and drugs, bad eating habits, artificial and crude behavior.

Manipura or Solar Chakra

It is situated at the level of the solar plexus on the inner wall of the spine, just behind the navel. The Sanskrit word *manipura* means 'city of jewels'. Its presiding deities are Lord Vishnu and Goddess Lakshmi.

Positively, it represents righteousness, dharma (sustenance), desire for evolution, welfare and wealth. It advocates the Ten Commandments as the guideline for self-realisation. Negatively, it represents involvement in domestic problems, dominance over spouse, either fasting or too much interest in food and material wealth.

Anahata or Heart Chakra

It lies at the inner wall of the spine just behind the centre of the chest. It is connected to the cardiac plexus and that part of the brain which is responsible for creativity and fine arts. Anahata means 'unstruck', that is, on awakening, the unstruck cosmic sound – AUM or LOGOS or WORD, which is created without the striking of two objects, is heard through inner ears, when all the internal noises of the mind have been silenced through sustained practices. Its presiding deities are Lord Shiva and Goddess Parvati.

In the positive sense it represents existence, love, truth and truth-attention-joy (sat-chit-ananda). In the negative sense it represents extreme physical and mental activities, bad relations (especially with the mother), indulgence in drugs, no faith in God and anti-God activities. Aura balancing can remove some negativity.

Vishuddhi or Throat Chakra

It is located at the juncture of the spine and medulla oblongata, in the cervical plexus directly behind the throat pit. Its presiding deity is Lord Krishna with Goddess Radha, who is the eternal witness, watching the cosmic drama with complete detachment. Literally it means 'centre of purification'.

Positively, it suggests witnessing of the Self. Negatively, it indicates mortality, guilt, sarcastic attitude, foul tongue, smoking, problems of cold and bronchial tubes – such as sinus, snoring and panting.

Through balancing one can get over these negative aspects.

Ajna or Eyebrow Chakra

It is located at the top of the spinal chord, at the medulla oblongata, and is connected to the pineal gland. Purification of the pineal guarantees the proper functioning of pituitary and other glands and thus the chakra takes care of the whole body. The presiding deity of the central chakra is Lord Jesus Christ – representing forgiveness and resurrection, that of the left chakra is Lord Mahavira – representing subconscious (superego), and the deity of the right chakra is Lord Buddha – representing ahankar (ego). Ajna is the most important of the psychic centres. It is also known as 'centre of command', 'eye of Shiva', 'guru chakra', 'third eye', etc. It is the 'gateway to liberation'.

The positive aspects of the centre are sight, hearing and thought, and the negative aspects are bad association and wandering eyes. The positive aspects of the left are memories and conditioning from the past, and the negative aspects are addictions and self-indulgence. The positive aspects of the right are

I-ness, and the negative aspects are worries, harmful attitude towards others and incorrect notions of God. Balancing can get over these negative aspects to some extent.

Sahasrara or Crown Chakra

It is not actually a chakra since it exists above the head in a non-physical form, while any other chakra is within the realm of psyche and is connected to a plexus or a set of nerves. Sahasrara is the culmination of the journey of Kundalini, and the end result of all yoga practices. It has infinite virtues and can at best be represented by a thousand petalled lotus; hence the name sahasrara, meaning 'one thousand'. It is represented by a halo around the head of saints and liberated people. When Shakti and Shiva unite, the process of self-realisation begins as a series of experiences. One's identity is lost — the seer, seeing, and seen are merged into one 'single awareness'.

Positively, it means going beyond the duality and above the three states of being or gunas, called tamas (inertia), rajas (activity) and sattva (purity). Negatively, it means disbelief in God. In practical terms it would mean lacking the joy of life, and appearing withdrawn and aloof. Through balancing, these negative aspects can be taken care of to a good extent.

There is an additional chakra called *Bindu* between Ajna and Sahasrara, situated at the crown of the head. It is at a point where Hindus tie a tuft of hair, called 'shikha' in Sanskrit. Bindu and Vishuddhi are internally connected through nerves. As such, bindu awakens automatically when vishuddhi awakens. Nectar flows from bindu and drips in vishuddhi, wherefrom it spreads into the whole body. It arrests the ageing process and causes rejuvenation.

Balancing the Aura

Location of the chakras with the help of a pendulum has been discussed already. You will find that the degrees to which various chakras are awakened in a person, are different. Also, the degree to which a particular chakra is awakened in different persons is different. When a chakra is not properly awakened, the person will be found to be in the grip of the negative aspects of that chakra. He/she may not be making proper use of the potential related to that chakra. Such a chakra can be rectified to a good extent by the pendulum, so that the person can make use of the related potential.

You can make a pendulum of your own or buy one from the market. You may find that some pendulums work better for you than others. You can also get an 'aura pendulum' on which colours are depicted, and the indicator can slide and be fixed at the particular colour you are dowsing for. After choosing the suitable pendulum, programme it for clear 'yes' and 'no' indications.

After talking to the subconscious and the pendulum, you can wait and watch. The pendulum will react and move after some time. It is advisable to check every now and again the directions indicating 'yes', and 'no', which are found to change in some cases.

If the pendulum depicts colours, set the indicator on red, if it does not, say to yourself that you are now checking the root chakra. Hold the pendulum by the index finger and thumb, and suspend it above the root chakra of the person lying in front of you. Now you should ask the pendulum whether the root chakra of the person is in good shape. Whatever the answer, make a note of it. Now move to the next and in this manner survey all the seven chakras and note their respective conditions. Come back to the chakra, which was not in good health. Ask the pendulum once again, "What is the condition of this chakra?" Like this, survey the chakras, which are not in good shape, once again to be sure. Then go to each bad chakra again and, stopping at each one, ask the pendulum, "Is this the most negative chakra?" Find out about the chakra which needs maximum attention at this moment.

Now ask the pendulum about the directions indicating negative energies and positive energies, so that you are sure of it before starting the balancing. Then keep a glass of water on the table and dip the fingers of the other hand, which is not holding the pendulum, in it. Hold the pendulum on the chakra that needs maximum attention now, and ask the pendulum to extract the negative energies from it. In a while the pendulum will start moving in the direction of negative energies. It is now extracting the negative energy from the chakra, which is travelling through the pendulum into your body and finally getting dissolved into water. When the pendulum stops, you can take your hand out of the water and wash it well in running tap water. In a similar manner, extract negative energy from all the chakras, one by one. You can keep talking to the person during the experiment and ask him the possible reason for this negativity. He/she might come out with the explanation, perhaps in a regretful mood, and this will help in washing out the negativity faster.

Check again all the chakras to make sure that they show positive signs. If not, you may have to do the balancing for some of the chakras again. It is better to finish off with a green coloured pendulum moving in a positive direction over all the chakras. This will give a final healing touch to the person concerned. You will notice that the pendulum has become your friend in many ways and you may like to travel with it all the time.

Another way to balance the energy is through crystals. There are crystals available in almost all colours; you should choose the one suited to your ailing chakra, in particular. A quartz crystal helps all the chakras in general. Remember that the crystals absorb the energy, negative or positive, and reflect it back to you. So if you spend time with people having negative habits, the crystal will gradually pass on their negativity to you. Being with good energy people, positive energy will be strengthening you from time to time. It is good to wear the crystal such that it touches your skin somewhere. Having returned from a place of negative energy, the crystal should be washed with its knob down in clear water for a few seconds.

True Meaning of Colours

Traditionally a particular colour would typify a person and say, "this is how the person is". True meaning would differ on the 'level of certainty' and say, "this is how the person should be". This is so because only a few of us live or are able to live correctly according to the traditional meaning. Most of us do not live or are not able to live the way the traditional meaning expects. This observation applies equally to astrology, numerology, palm reading predictions, etc.

According to the traditional meaning nature normally offers an opportunity to people, which they fail to grab for several reasons. One of the most common reasons is the fear of failing. In some corner of their heart they feel that this is what they are supposed to be, and perhaps they could have done it. However, they were afraid, and the opportunity passed by. They felt safer in leading a mediocre life. I personally am aware of missing several grand opportunities that came my way.

The other prominent reason for missing the opportunity is to live as a means to an end. People have to earn money to pay the bills and run the family, and so, they cannot pursue the special lines offered by their primary colour. They could have become extraordinary, but they were forced by circumstances to live a mediocre life. More often than not such people are painfully aware of what they have missed. But, I repeat, the opportunities keep persisting, and at any other time in life you can still seize one of them. You always have a chance to live true to the traditional meaning of the colour.

Thus, an engineer, a doctor, a lecturer, a carpenter, a blacksmith, a cobbler – all may be having the same colour as primary in the aura, but they are leading different professions. Similarly, if you see the auras of half a dozen librarians, for example, you may be surprised to see that they have six different colours as primary in their auras. This explains why most people are doing what they are not supposed to be doing. Yet there are a few who are doing what they are supposed to be doing. And they are the brilliant ones, known in society for their work. Galileo, Einstein, Rabindranath Tagore, Gurdjief, Martin Luther King, Nat King Cole are some such examples. This should motivate you to find your primary colour in the aura, and to live up to its requirements, if possible. It is never too late.

Then there are mood colours in the auras. For example, if you are angry or jealous or revengeful, a dirty red can appear in the outskirts of your aura. Murderers and condemned people may have dull red and black combined at the moment of their intense feelings.

When you are in love or in a peaceful state or involved in religious activities, blue and violet may appear in the aura. Blue and green appearing together may imply intuitive awareness. Appearance of grey would mean depression or stress. When you are thoughtful, a yellow tinge may be seen in the outskirts. When you are involved in philanthropic or compassionate activities, indigo may be seen in the aura for that time. These are temporary appearances. However, the traditional meanings of colours are given below.

Traditional Meanings of Colours

Red	Leadership, energy, aggressiveness
Orange	Peace, cooperation, diplomacy, health
Yellow	Creative expression, joy of living, intellect
Green	Order, service, healing, construction
Blue	Constructive freedom, travel, resourcefulness, love of knowledge and sex
Indigo	Balance, responsibility, humanitarianism, love, domesticity

Violet	Analysis, understanding, intuition, spirituality, clairvoyance
Pink	Materialism, attainment, execution, love of power and position
Bronze	Selflessness, philanthropy, tolerance, compassion
Silver	Illumination, intuition, vision, impracticality
Gold	Master builder

Health and Aura-protection

Closest to the body is that part of the aura which one sees in the beginning. It represents health, good or bad. For good health the aura glows with brightness and vitality and it may even appear as rays of light going out. Negative thoughts and ill health result in inflammation, dark spots and distortion in the aura, long before the appearance of the disease in physical form. One can take clues from there and advise the person of a potential unhealthy situation. One can relate the part of the aura that is irregular with the corresponding part of the physical body. You can warn about the likelihood of some disease, without claiming for sure, since that is the job of the medical doctor. You can advise him/her to go in for a medical check-up and diagnosis by a doctor. A disease can be arrested before it manifests itself in physical form, through the study of aura.

A turned-in aura indicates lack of energy and pain in the related part of the body. Alternatively, a grey smudge may appear before the person is affected. For example, before someone gets a bronchial problem, the area around the chest may show a grey smudge. If the pain becomes chronic, the aura may shrink permanently, the colours may turn dull and a black spot may appear at the area of pain. For any chronic illness, the related part of the aura turns greyish brown. If the muscles are torn or damaged, the aura may develop holes in it. On the return of a healthy situation, the holes disappear. In general, grey, brown, dark or dull red and black are warnings of serious ill health or a chronic disease. If someone has radiant lines during good health, the lines may become asymmetrical, inflammated or discoloured and/or their size may be reduced to nearly half or one-third when they are ill.

A mental and spiritual process can always be used to heal a person. The tiredness or fatigue in a person can be removed by bathing him/her in a stream of bright red light by the healer. This can be followed by a flush of rich yellow or warm orange light. Bathing him/her in a stream of blue or violet light can invigorate the person. Finally the person should be bathed in white light, which will generate in the person an illuminated state of mind and soul and the healer himself will get charged with cosmic energy. A depressed person can come out of his/her depression through repeated bathing in bright pink light by the healer. Many healers in Florida have been known to heal people through a rush of mixed white and blue light. Eating coloured food items also restores the deficiency of colours in the aura.

In my yoga and meditation workshops, I end by inviting liquid white light which enters into the body through the crown centre. I ask the participants to visualise a globe of light at each of the seven chakras.

Then the people are asked to feel the presence of liquid white light everywhere inside and outside their bodies. Then they are asked to feel the presence of the divine hand on top of their head, from which energy and vibrations emanate and enter their bodies. This is called *shaktipat*. Most people report the vanishing of fatigue or pain from any part of the body and invigoration of the whole body. A regular workshop of two hours every day can repair the aura of its deficiencies and protect it from all ill-effects permanently. Yogis live in perfect health and they never bother to see the colours of the aura.

However, for an average person the following practices are helpful:

- A dull red points to energy being down.

  Remedies: Physical exercises; regular walks for 15-20 minutes, twice a day; participation in games and sports. The company of positive-minded and successful people helps to get stimulation and encouragement.

- A weak orange is a sign of poor cooperative spirit and feelings of frustration.

  Remedies: Find pleasure in helping others and caring for

others without expecting any returns.

- A dull yellow means that you are not enjoying life and are not involved in any kind of creative activity.

  Remedies: Begin to study a subject that attracts you. Pick up hobbies or some profession where you can use your unique gift of words; use humour whenever you find an opportunity.

- A waning green colour is a sign of lacking in compassion and being unhelpful.

Remedies: Cash in on opportunities for helping and healing others, for example, giving tuition to a friend's child without remuneration, buying medicines for the neighbour, spending time with people who need your presence, etc.

- If you are not enjoying adventure, creative activities, a search for knowledge, love and sex, and public relations, then your primary blue is at stake.

  Remedies: Avoid wasting time in cheap pleasures, do not scatter energy by having too many irons in the fire, avoid impatience and restlessness and try to achieve perfection in one line of action.

- If you are not finding interest in humanitarian and philanthropic activities, your primary indigo may be losing brightness.

  Remedies: Rely on your feelings, trust others, do not criticise yourself or others, for you are not the only one responsible for what is happening, and find an outlet through some creative activity.

- If you are not self-reliant and are involved in philosophic or spiritual activities, your primary violet may be fading in its glory.

Remedies: Do not hold back. Try to communicate with others. Others may not like your philosophical approach. Become more adaptable by knowing the needs of others.

- If you are dependent on others, if others are putting the blame on you and you are feeling the pressure of things; things are not right with your primary pink.

  Remedies: Cultivate a new interest and do something which you have had in mind for a long time. Give up timidity, develop confidence in yourself, and share your work-load with others, even if you have to be hard on them.

- If others are taking advantage of your helping and humanitarian nature and if you are feeling negative, then your primary bronze may be losing its shine.

  Remedies: Withdraw from being too involved in others' work, and find some time for yourself. However, serving others selflessly and without return has unimaginable rewards from nature.

- If you lack imagination, self-confidence and inspiration, and are incapable of seeing good in others, your primary silver may be lifeless.

Remedies: Trust your virtues of intuition and self-respect, give a practical shape to your imaginative plans and bring some good results. Learn to relax through yoga and meditation.

- If you are finding it difficult to use your infinite capabilities for completing the project in hand, your primary gold may be weak.

  Remedies: Do not expect too much from yourself as compared to others, and stop being hard on yourself. Remember that, "to err is human." Learn from mistakes and move ahead.